AF225611

From Horror to Hope

A child's survival in the midst of torture and death.

Judena Klebs

Copyright © 2013 by Judena Klebs
All rights reserved.
ISBN-10: 1494223767
ISBN-13: 978-1494223762

This book is dedicated to all who helped Lisa come from "Horror to Hope".

Introduction

This is a true story. However, many names have been changed. Though written in a creative manner, it does not depart from the facts. Some of Lisa's memories may seem difficult to believe. Many people are not aware of the true activities that take place undercover in the occult.

Lisa bears in her body evidences of the torture she endured. Can it be proven? Like the existence of God, the evidence is there but cannot be proven either way.

Some parts of Lisa's story may seem controversial, such as deliverance from evil spirits or dissociation and multiple personalities. Yet the spiritual world and that of the mind are not usually explored thoroughly until trauma makes it necessary.

The story of Lisa's journey is not meant to repulse the reader or to entertain, but to bring hope to all who have suffered emotional anguish or may be suffering it now. If it brings change, healing, and hope to those who read it, Lisa's struggles will not be in vain. If it brings insight to those who desire to be helpful, let its purpose be fulfilled.

Chapter One

The air was still damp and crisp, as it had been the evening before. Small hands dug in the mud among the soggy leaves from rain and dew that had come overnight.

The sobbing two-year-old dug her fingers deeper into the ground. Pain under her fingernails was sharp. Yet it was hardly noticeable because of the pain in her heart.

Little Lisa dug feverishly and in a panic. If only she could change what she had witnessed the night before.

Somehow Little Lisa had broken away from the crowd of people who were still sleeping on the ground, not far from this scene. She had been held captive by them, and yet tore away from their camp so early in the morning.

Lisa's thoughts went back to the night before when the knife came down upon her baby brother. Blood had been spilled and he lay silent. She searched for him now where she had seen them bury him. Wasn't this the spot she had gazed at the evening before, when she determined to bring him back and to erase the terrible memory? She would rescue and bring him back to life somehow.

No matter how deeply she dug, the body was not there. The truth was that the body had been moved and Lisa did not know where. The hope of changing what she had seen was now gone and it was *her fault*. If she had died instead, the infant would not have had to be killed. Isn't that what they had told her? She gave up crying and digging.

Now Little Lisa had to forget what happened and "Bad Girl" took her place. Little Lisa was now gone and could go back to childhood as though this had not taken place. "Bad Girl" took the memory away with her and Little Lisa completely forgot about what had caused her pain. She went back and joined the group, woke up again and showed no emotional sign of having been away.

However, her clothes were wet and a few leaves still clung to her legs. Her fingernails were swollen and stained with mud. The adults would not notice this for they hardly noticed Lisa was there until it was time to torture her body and mind again.

To Little Lisa, this was just another thing to forget and she ignored any physical signs, too, that she had been away. It would be many years before this memory would resurface and her pain felt again.

Chapter Two

Someone had apparently loved Little Lisa when she was first born to give her a name like Larisa Dawn. Not only was it a unique and beautiful name but the meaning of her middle name "Dawn" seemed to celebrate the new life.

Who had named her such a thoughtful name? Most would have expected it to be her mother. And so it seemed to be the case. Yet Lisa would find out someday that the name must have come from God, Himself, who saw a meaning in Lisa's life even from the start.

Lisa remembered her mother rocking her in the rocking chair, singing to her. She remembered an original impression that, somewhere, there might be meaning in the world as her mother sang.

But then, Baby Lisa remembered the sound of yelling and her body being stiffened by fear as the male voice sounded throughout the house in a terrifying tone. She felt no sense of safety even in her crib as she heard the sound of the voice coming through the wall and felt a chill of horror whenever the man entered her room.

Lisa was able to depend on her mother for some of her physical needs or she would not have been able to survive. And, even in babyhood, some of those experiences were positive. The one thing she noticed, however, was that the older she became, the more her mother started to resent her for not being as helpless as she had been before.

Lisa became more and more aware of her mother's resentment and verbal assaults directed at her as she grew older. She longed for a mother who would give her approval and not just meet her physical needs.

"You'll never have any friends!", Lisa's mother, Gail, shouted. "If I had known you would be like this, I never would have had you!"

Lisa also was discovered to have an unusual talent in music which her mother envied. As Lisa grew older and could compose music on the piano, her mother noticed the talent and finally allowed Lisa to take piano lessons. Gail would hear Lisa play and then realized she could show her off to guests in her home.

"Play the piano, Lisa!" Gail ordered.

Lisa knew her mother just wanted to brag about the fact that she had given birth to a "genius" as she referred to Lisa. Lisa did not want to be put on display. She felt used. But even more than that she would suffer her mother's jealous "put-downs" after the company went away.

"You are not good enough!" her mother would scold.

Lisa knew that it was really her mother who felt that she, herself, was not "good enough", not to be able to play the piano and compose as Lisa did.

Chapter Three

"Where's my man?!" the 18-month old Lisa cried out in church.

Even though the parents were involved in occult activities behind the scenes, they attended church. One Sunday evening, a guest speaker was visiting the church while the pastor was away. Lisa, who apparently had developed an attachment to the regular pastor, awoke from sleep. Hearing a different voice and seeing an unfamiliar figure preaching from the pulpit, Lisa had cried out loudly.

Lisa would inwardly cry, "Where's my man?" throughout her life. This would cause much misunderstanding and embarrassment as she realized that she was not allowed to be attached to a man and her cry for a father would continue on and on.

There was always the yelling and frightening presence of the man the rest of the family called "Daddy". This man, also called Richard, began to take the two- and then, three- year- old "Little Lisa" out at night to "meetings". Sometimes the mother was there also and sometimes not. Many other adults and children were there, too, but Little Lisa did not see her two older sisters there. There was chanting and there were strange ceremonies. Many times blood from animals and humans was seen.

Little Lisa split into many other parts containing various memories. Like the branches of a tree, new twigs grew into her system of personalities containing the horror she witnessed.

It was "Bad Girl", a personality who split off from Little Lisa, who bore the memory of baby brother and being blamed for his death. Bad Girl would act out, but the memory of baby brother and all about him was locked away inside of her. She could not bear even to think about it or to remember him.

Lisa would feel depression and not know what it was or where it came from. The violence and death were locked away tightly inside Bad Girl's mind as she witnessed killing after endless killing.

The Bible was read in a cruel way. And prayer that was elaborate and phony filled the air. Even Little Lisa was forced to pray as a punishment.

"Repent, for you are evil! Lisa, you pray!", the cruel voice resounded., "You are the one who needs it!"

Terrible resentment toward Richard, the leader of this clan of people, who was also Lisa's father, filled Lisa's mind and heart. She wanted him dead before he could hurt anyone again. And this horrible Bible that he read in his cruel, snarling voice? Lisa hated it, too.

The unending mental torture, called "prayer", that Lisa was commanded to participate in as a condemnation for her wickedness brought a barrier against the God to whom she was forced to pray. She hated that "God" as well.

Chapter Four

The church, where Lisa's parents attended, had a basement where terrible rituals were performed at night. Lisa's father, who had a key to the building, let his followers enter there to perform their rituals of torture.

The basement also had a Sunday-school room off to the side. This was the three-and four-year-old class that Lisa attended on Sunday mornings.

One Sunday morning, Lisa's class traced and learned a verse of Scripture, "God is love." All the children colored their papers to take them home.

"What is love?" Lisa thought. "There is no such thing! So there must be no such thing as this God, either." This was Lisa's philosophy for many years to come. She would explain to herself that the God she hated didn't really exist anyway.

"You naughty girl! You got blood all over your dress!" Lisa scolded.

The words sounded like a heartless reprimand to her older sister, Jill. It was really "Bad Girl" speaking.

The mother, Gail, was angry. Lisa's oldest sister, Brenda, was angry, too. The family thought that Lisa was a cruel and evil child. How could a three-year-old say such a thing to her sister?

Five year old, Jill, had fallen out of a tree that she had been climbing. She was brought into the house, wounded and bloody. An ambulance was called to take her to the hospital. Lisa was very frightened to see Jill bleeding. A part of Lisa that remembered blood being associated with shame spilled out of her in her fear.

Lisa, herself, had been blamed for blood, both her own and others. Now she used what she had been told about herself during the rituals as a weapon to project onto her sister. She immediately hated herself for what she had just said. Yet it somehow made sense, coming out of her experiences. If she was naughty and responsible for her own bleeding, wasn't she justified to make her sister responsible, who had climbed the tree without permission.

Perhaps Jill would die (and Lisa could not cope with that) so she must blame her for the blood and push her out of her life emotionally. "Bad Girl" had to find expression and make someone else bad for once. The guilt she held for bleeding and causing others to bleed was unbearable. At last, someone was bleeding outside the rituals, someone whom Lisa could put some of that guilt upon. Someone she trusted and loved the most. Someone she feared would suffer and die like Baby Brother.

Jill survived but Lisa's comment was held against her by Brenda who continued to resent Lisa throughout her life for being "spoiled" and "cruel"! She did not understand Lisa's problem.

There was a big move to another, larger city when Lisa was three-and one-half years old. With the move, the rituals dropped away for a while. Yet abuse at home continued.

One sunny day at preschool, four-year-old Lisa took the paint-brush and can of water from Miss Gardner. This was Lisa's favorite play thing to do during recess. Paint with water!

As creatively as ever, Lisa began to paint the patio and sidewalk of the playground area. Houses, trees, animals, circles, squares. On and on she painted, not really stopping to look back at the results too much.

Then it came again. That gnawing ache inside her chest and head, the unsatisfied hunger for love. As Lisa stopped her work, she saw how quickly the sun had destroyed her creations. The futile feelings of her life came over her. Somehow, the disappearance of her works of art represented the uselessness of her life.

The emptiness of it all brought gloom and heartache to Lisa. That feeling would be there throughout her life, that useless, overwhelming pain of depression and emptiness.

While she pondered how her paintings and all meaning in life had been destroyed by the merciless sun, storm-clouds were gathering in Lisa's emotional sky as she approached the age of five. The Satanic rituals would begin again.

In the meantime, there was still cruelty at home, and unhappy Lisa tried over and over again to run away and find peace. For some reason, Lisa did not allow the fact to be registered in her mind that if she chose the same place over and over again to run away to, she would be found.

      The orchard was not far from Lisa's neighborhood. She ran along a dirt path where she could sneak toward the orange tree grove. There she could sit down on the dirt and in the grass and clover. She would pretend that all was safe in her world. For a few minutes, she would bask in the balance of sun and shade, picking small, blue flowers that were growing abundantly across the dirt. This was her world. She escaped the hurt and rejection from parents for a very short time. Then Lisa was punished severely for running away when she was found. Yet she kept coming to the same place, her own pleasant place to find for a few minutes. The orchard caused Lisa to dream of what life could perhaps be someday. She day-dreamed of peace. The orchard was the one window into her make-believe world of hope and tranquility.

Chapter Five

The slab of stone was cold and rough. Lisa laid as still as she could, but her naked body shivered in the cold breeze. Lisa knew that another vaginal stabbing would take place to produce blood as a part of the rituals. She must lay still or the torture would grow worse as a punishment for not accepting her fate of suffering.

After that point, Lisa no longer remembered what had occurred, for a new personality formed to take that trauma and lock it away. The world, and even Lisa herself, would not remember until her mind was ready.

There had been stabbings, hangings, and people's hearts being cut out. Each time these traumas occurred, a different part of Lisa's brain took a part of the memories so that Lisa, herself, could escape mental insanity. More and more branches to the "family tree" of Lisa's personalities grew from the five-year old.

A personality named "Stab" took the stabbings in Lisa's vagina. Another, called "Dead" believed she was dead after being buried alive, dug up, and told that she was dead.

Lisa has the scar of a stab wound near her heart where they tried to cut her heart out while it was still beating. The person performing the ritual missed her heart, putting him in risk of death, himself, for not performing the ritual successfully. This was the meaning of burying Lisa to bring her back and pretend she was somebody else! By this time, Lisa *was* somebody else in her own mind. Whenever "Dead" came out, Lisa would say to her friends,

"I am Dead."

"You can't be dead or you wouldn't be talking to me." they would say.

Her friends didn't understand that Lisa's personality from burial was introducing herself to them. Her name was "Dead".

All this time, Lisa was a very shy, fearful child in kindergarten. By the time she got to first grade, she had strange patterns to her behavior.

"You don't like me!" Lisa cried.

While playing on the playground with her friend, Cathy, she would get an awful sense of rejection and fear for seemingly no reason, then run away and hide. Her friend would find her crying and ask her why.

"You don't like me!" Lisa would say.

After reassuring Lisa that she did like her, Cathy would get her friend to go back to play. Then the whole episode would be repeated.

Through the trauma at age five, Lisa had lost all awareness of her own pain and her cry for love. The sense of rejection and hopelessness which kept her from playing normally also caused her to act out at home. Her sisters thought she was simply a spoiled "problem child".

Over time, Lisa came to realize that some of her fear was that she would lose the kind people in her life by accepting their love. Where was this particular fear coming from? The answer would be found in another locked-up memory.

Chapter Six

	"Grab him!" Richard shouted.
The surrounding men hurried to obey his every wish.
"Cut him!" the monster-man roared again.
	Blades of knives began to appear all around the group.
Flying from every direction, they aimed the knives at the man who
had been kind to the children.
	Long after becoming an adult and working through her
therapy, Lisa remembered a man in the cult being kind and talking
to the children. He had then been punished by being butchered
alive in the presence of the children.
	"This is what happens when you let someone be kind
to you!" Richard hollered at the children.
	Lisa would protect others from being kind to her by
rejecting their efforts to reach out to her in kindness. She didn't
dare watch them get hurt or possibly violently killed. So she
created a personality needed to drive people away from her. "Bad-
As-Can-Be" came out viciously, fighting every effort of others to
love or be kind to her or to communicate that love in any way. This
meant that she would act as bad as she could but also hurt inwardly
as bad as possible, for she longed desperately for the love she
rejected and feared.
	About this time, six-year-old Lisa had been attending a
Sunday School class at the new church the family attended. When
the teacher began to teach on baptism, one sentence the teacher
said grabbed a hold on Lisa's heart.
	"When you are baptized, it means that you have
become one of God's own special children." the teacher stated.
	Lisa's face paled as she realized that this was what she
had been longing for all of her life. To be someone's own special
child! To be loved, to be wanted! If only she could be important
enough to someone that they would give her the attention for
which she cried. The hunger in her heart burned and she was
determined to find this specialness. She could think of nothing
else.
	Lisa asked her pastor if he would baptize her. He then
spoke to her parents.

"I don't believe that Lisa really understands what baptism is about. And she is only six."

The pastor was right that she did not understand, but Lisa was determined to become God's own special child. She insisted and was baptized.

Life, then, went on the same. No love. If she had become anyone's special child, she could not sense it. There was no one to treat her as though she was special. No one to take her in their arms and comfort her, no one to wash the hurt away. Lisa had gone into the water and out of the water just as hungry for love as ever. Her greatest longing was once again beyond her reach for fulfillment.

Chapter Seven

A beautiful girl, named Sharon, skipped happily and perfectly over each turn of the rope. Her friends cheered her on.

Everyone loved Sharon. She was completely surrounded by the smiles of the children her age. Sharon wore a pretty, lacy, red dress with a pure, white collar and sleeves. No one could even compare to her beauty and grace.

After jumping rope, the other children surrounded Sharon once again. Love and admiration shone upon her from these friends as they continued on to play Tether Ball, Hopscotch, Hide and Seek, and then to build mountains and castles in the sandbox.

Sharon was the most valued and loved child among her playmates. No one ever got angry at her. Then where was the shouting, angry voice coming from?

"Why are you daydreaming and not doing your work!" Miss Jones' voice filled the classroom.

Lisa awoke to the angry glare of her fourth-grade teacher. Sharon had disappeared.

Terribly frightened, Lisa became more and more angry, herself, as the woman yelled at her in front of all the other children in the class.

"Go to the corner and stay there!" Miss Jones shouted.

Completely humiliated, Lisa buried her head in the corner of the room. What had she done? Why was Miss Jones so angry at her? Why were people always yelling and expressing such hatred toward her?

Lisa remembered nothing she had done wrong. She was not aware of the school paper that had been placed on her desk at some point during class. Where did Sharon go? Where was the popular, beautiful girl who was loved?

Chapter Eight

It was a hot day. Eleven-year-old Lisa had not walked far from her school on her way home. Yet the heat bore down upon her and she had a long way to travel home with her school books.

Lisa noticed a truck pulling over as she walked along the sidewalk. As she grew closer, she recognized the man in the driver's seat. Her next-door neighbor had recently moved away and there he was, asking her if she wanted a ride home.

Lisa remembered Mr. Wiley and the time he would spend with the children in the neighborhood when no one else would pay attention to them. He would give them "horsy rides" in the front lawn of his house.

Though the teachers had warned Lisa, along with the other children, not to accept rides from strangers, this man certainly was no stranger to Lisa. No grown-up had ever paid so much attention to her. She was flattered that he would offer her a ride home in this hot weather.

Lisa accepted the ride and asked the man why he was back in town near where he had lived. He replied that he was looking at vacant houses in order to find another place to live.

Lisa chatted to her friend as he drove toward her house. He, then, pulled over about five blocks before reaching the neighborhood where they both had lived.

"There is a vacant house I need to look at here." he said.

Lisa was invited to get out of the car to look at the house with him. They approached the door and it was locked.

Then Mr. Wiley asked Lisa to go into the shed with him to look at it. Lisa entered with him. They had just entered and looked around a short time.

"Let me give you a horsy ride." Mr. Wiley said.

Surprised, Lisa complied and allowed him to pick her up. At first the "horsy ride" was the same as always. Then Mr. Wiley began to act strangely. Lisa was used to strange things being done to her and yet she was very frightened. She knew, however, that she must always allow adults to have their way and became passive as a rag doll in Mr. Wiley's hands.

The next time Mr. Wiley came down the street near her school, offering her a ride home, Lisa hesitated because he had acted so strangely the first time. However, he had eventually taken her home, so she was embarrassed not to accept. Perhaps he really wanted to be her friend. How she longed for someone to be her friend and to accept and love her as a child! Maybe this time he would just talk to her and take her directly home. He may no longer need to look at vacant houses. So Lisa accepted. Then she noticed Mr. Wiley turn a corner. Where was he going this time?

"I need to look at another vacant house." he said.

Now Lisa was becoming more frightened than before. Why was Mr. Wiley looking at vacant houses each time he picked her up?

The house where Mr. Wiley took Lisa was even further from her neighborhood. It was an unfinished house right next to a field. Other houses were quite far from the field and were facing the opposite direction.

Mr. Wiley parked in the field right next to the house. Once again, he asked Lisa to go into the house with him and look at it, but why was he stopping at a low brick wall before getting to the house?

"Let me give you a horsy ride." Mr. Wiley said, as before.

Lisa did not want a horsy ride, but she had learned never to question what adults asked her to do. Mr. Wiley picked her up. This time he held her tight. His hands really hurt her and she tried not to show it. Lisa had learned to endure pain brought upon her by adults without letting them know. This had always kept her safer from further abuse in the past, for her father became more intent on increasing the pain whenever Lisa cried or showed any sign that she was hurt.

Finally, Mr. Wiley stopped manipulating Lisa's body and let her out of his grip. He began to walk toward the house.

"Walk with me around the side of the house." Mr. Wiley said.

Then he picked her up again to hold her up to the window. Again his grip was tight.

Over and over, Mr. Wiley gripped and lifted Lisa. Then he wanted her to enter the house with him by a side, unfinished wall.

The house was an empty shell and nothing to really look at, yet Mr. Wiley kept Lisa there, continuing to manipulate her body. Would he ever take her home?

Fear and confusion filled Lisa's body and mind. Why was she here? She had wanted a friend, yet this man was doing strange things to her and did not seem eager to let her go.

Finally, Mr. Wiley led Lisa out of the house, back to the brick wall in the back of the house. Once again, he picked her up, set her on the brick wall, and then gripped her again, hurting her. The painful manipulating of Lisa's body was finally interrupted by a man walking toward them across the field. The man took Mr. Wiley aside to talk to him. Lisa walked over to Mr. Wiley's truck.

"Let's get out of here!" Mr. Wiley said with fear in his voice, as he climbed into the truck.

Lisa hurried to get into the truck, sensing the fear in Mr. Wiley's voice, and wondering what he was afraid might happen to them. Before Mr. Wiley could pull the truck out of the field, the man who had talked to him came over to the driver's window.

"Is this man your father?" the man asked Lisa, looking across at her.

"No"

Lisa told the truth, although she wondered if this had been the right thing to do for she continued to sense Mr. Wiley's fear. The new man encouraged Lisa out of the truck.

"Come over and talk to my wife at my house." the man said.

Lisa was led to the front of a house where a woman greeted her and welcomed her in. The woman invited her to sit down.

"My husband told me to call the police." the woman said.

What had Lisa done?!

"My husband is a former police officer.", the woman explained. "He told me that he didn't like the way that man was holding you."

Soon the woman's husband came back and brought

Lisa back into the field, where a police officer was talking to both Mr. Wiley and to the man who had intervened. Another police officer, whom Lisa had not seen at first, told Lisa to get into his police car.

Lisa got into the car. Fear gripped her heart, mind, and body like never before.

"Why am I in trouble? What have I done? Did I get Mr. Wiley in some kind of trouble?" Lisa asked herself.

Lisa tried to remember what terrible thing she had done wrong. All she could remember was wanting Mr. Wiley to be her friend, to pay attention to her.

While Lisa waited inside the police car, she felt a fear that God, Himself, would punish her severely for what terrible thing she had done. She should never have wanted to be loved.

Lisa begged God not to send her to the hell that she had heard about in church. She expected to descend there at any moment. Never had she experienced so much fear!

As the police officer entered the car and began to drive away with Lisa, she felt so ashamed for the crime she had done. Wanting to be loved by a man was, somehow, the worst thing Lisa had ever done. The silence was finally broken by the police officer's question.

"What grade are you in?" he asked.

Confusion filled Lisa again. How could the police officer ask her something like that while he drove her to her doom, whatever that doom would be?!

"Sixth grade", Lisa whispered.

Chapter Nine

No more was said, as the police officer drove Lisa to the police station. When they arrived, Lisa was taken to a very small room and told to wait.

"What will they do to me?" Lisa cried to herself.

One by one, various police officers came in to ask Lisa questions that she did not know how to answer. She was more afraid and confused as they asked her about Mr. Wiley and what he had done to her body. The shame and embarrassment built even more, the longer she was made to wait. The total fear and the begging God for mercy continued.

Finally, a policeman allowed Lisa to leave the room and she saw her parents and brother-in-law waiting for her. Lisa's brother-in-law looked embarrassed and intimidated by her parents. No one spoke. Pretty soon Lisa was ushered into the car and driven home. How Lisa wished that the silence would be interrupted with some kind of explanation for what had occurred! No explanation ever came.

Lisa's sin of wanting to be loved would always haunt her. She vowed to herself that she would never be guilty of such a sin again.

There were several things that the experience with Mr. Wiley came to mean to Lisa. How would she ever be wanted and loved by a father? What did men want from a daughter? What would please them? Lisa wanted someone to be excited in a positive way that she had come into the world, but so far the message had been that she should have died.

Also, Lisa was confused about what would really cause a father to desire her. The boys at school made fun of her for not dressing in the short dresses that were in style and adorned the other girls. Yet her father yelled at her if her dress was even an inch above her knees. What did boys and men want?

Someday, Lisa would be told that men would notice and be excited about her if she got involved in stripping and exotic dancing. Although Lisa never did actually do that, she harbored a desire to, perhaps someday, use that method to gain the love of men. She began to realize why so many women degrade themselves and gain the disgust of men. The life they get into, the way they dress, and the seductive ways that they have been taught are a last resort to find some form of love. If these women can't be loved, they are led to believe that perhaps they can, at least, be wanted, even if it is in a degrading way. For them, that would be better than not being wanted at all.

Children who have not been wanted or loved by parents are so desperate for even an inkling of the feeling of being desired, even if that desire is lustful and not a true love. It is better than nothing for them because of the desperate cry of their hearts. It is a hunger that will push them "over the edge" into an indecent life. Many men do not understand this and are critical of these women's motives.

"They are trying to seduce men!" they say, "How despicable!".

So these men reject the women and despise them further. Once again, these women's search for love is futile.

Also, women are sometimes taught by their culture that they must have perfect bodies in order to be loved or even accepted as human beings. They chase after weight loss, cosmetic perfection, and so on. They struggle to receive the love and admiration of men. Many times this only causes them to become even more of a "sex object" in the eyes of men.

Chapter Ten

The monstrous face was red and inhuman. It appeared as a vicious, hateful-looking animal, fierce and devilish.

Lisa was 13 years old. Why had her father, Richard, entered her bedroom? Lisa had no clue concerning his rage. She would never know what had caused him to storm into her room, change into the face of a vicious animal and head toward her while she lay in her bed. He grabbed her pillow and pushed it hard on her face.

"What do you want me to do?! Hate you? Kill you?" he hollered.

Lisa remembered no conflict that could have enraged him. She could no longer breathe and the truth that he was really trying to smother her sunk into her heart with a deep, agonizing pain. The reality of it hurt her so much that she hoped he would succeed and that she would die.

So that was what Lisa's father had wanted all along! Her death. That was the only thing that would ever please him and make him happy.

The next instant, Lisa was waking up in her room and the door was now closed. Her father was gone out of the room. As Lisa came out of unconsciousness, she cried a deep cry and determined to make Daddy happy someday through her death. This consumed her mind and heart from then on.

Why did Lisa only pass out and not smother completely? What had stopped Richard from killing her? Then she remembered that her mother had somehow intervened. This was amazing for it was the only time Lisa's mother showed any indication that she cared what was done to her. Lisa remembered now that her mother, Gail, had all of a sudden come out of the trance-like state that she seemed to live in and had even cried out to Richard.

"Rich, you are going to hurt her!" Gail had warned.

This was a shock to Lisa. Now she remembered how puzzled she felt to hear her mother have any concern for her. It must have been Gail who had stopped him from finishing the job.

After crying deeply, Lisa ventured to the door and

opened it. No one was around and later, when she walked through the house, everything was as before. No one spoke of the incident. All carried on their activities as if Lisa were not there.

Lisa thought of suicide as her destiny from then on. She would carry the wounds of people wanting her to die for the major part of her life. Her depression got so bad that she could barely function. School was difficult for her because she could not concentrate. She even had trouble paying attention during her music lessons.

During Junior High School, most of Lisa's schoolmates laughed at her and called her "ugly". Then the boys, and sometimes even the girls, began to attack Lisa physically. A group of boys would gather together and knock her over on the way to class. There was no relief or refuge for Lisa at home or at school. Her life was full of continuous fear.

When Lisa went to High School, things were slightly better in the way her classmates treated her. However, there were two teachers in Lisa's high school who taught evolution. For Lisa's first two years there, they taught that there was no God. Lisa had only a small thread of faith from what she had heard in church. As she listened to the mockery against Christian beliefs, Lisa lost all hope that there could be any meaning in life. There was either no God at all or He was the torturer that she had believed him to be from the beginning.

There was no meaning or purpose to life. Death, itself, became Lisa's only focus. She sunk into the deepest despair and a feeling of torment filled her mind and heart. What if there were a God and she was not capable of believing in him? She had heard that one must give his or her life to God to be saved from hell and to go to heaven. If Lisa were wrong about God, she would go to hell forever. This actually seemed, for Lisa, to be a fitting conclusion to a life of agony.

At a crusade that her parents attended with Lisa, a sermon was given about a woman who lived her life as though there was a God, gave her life to him, and when she was old, she knew that she would die and go to heaven. Lisa wanted to believe that this could be true for her, too.

"God," she said, " If you really are there, give me the faith to believe that you exist."

Suddenly, Lisa knew that God was real and she wanted to give her life to Him. What did she have to lose? A life that was worthless to her. As far as she was concerned, she was as "good as dead" already.

Lisa went down to the wooden altar set up in the pavilion that was being used for the crusade. She prayed quietly, making a commitment that her life from now on would belong to the God she had not been able to believe in before.

That night, when Lisa went to bed, she felt a strange sensation of a "tug of war" within her body. Something strong pulled her from one direction and another force pulled on her from the opposite side of her body and head. What was this war she was feeling? It was as if an argument about who she belonged to were taking place. From now on, every time Lisa tried to pray or read her Bible or to live for God in all the ways she thought she should, a force would be fighting her. It would put pressure against her and she would have to push hard to fight it off.

Lisa got up every morning and forced herself to read the Bible and say a short prayer. In spite of the awful depression she constantly felt, Lisa struggled to remind herself that she was now a Christian and had given her life completely to God.

Chapter Eleven

Gail had some concern for the daughter she seemed to despise, for she was willing to take her to a psychologist. She saw that Lisa could not function and knew she was smart enough to do her music and make better grades.

Dr. Carter gave Lisa psychological and intelligence tests. He then went over the results with her.

"You are very smart and gifted. You should be making straight A's in school." Dr. Carter said.

Dr. Carter referred Lisa to a psychiatrist who placed her on an anti-depressant. Then, for a time, Dr. Carter met with her once a month to check on her and counsel her.

One day, Dr. Carter called Lisa's parents in to visit with him along with Lisa. Richard and Gail were very nervous, especially Richard.

"What are they afraid of?" Lisa wondered.

"Whatever was done to you was not your fault." Dr. Carter stated to Lisa in front of her parents.

Lisa's father went wild, completely outraged that Dr. Carter would try to take blame off of Lisa. Lisa's mother became even more nervous than she had been, partly because she feared Richard's reaction.

Lisa was terrified that she would be punished for being told it was not her fault, yet suddenly she saw that there was something true about Dr. Carter's statements that terrified her father. If the things done to her were not her fault, then who was responsible?

The punishments that Lisa had endured within her family came about the same distance apart as always. She would be hit, yelled at, and once, had been shoved out of the car at the school parking lot. She was told, once again, that everything that had been done to her was definitely her fault.

However, the straight A's that Dr. Carter had predicted came to pass as Lisa gained energy while on the anti-depressant. She got involved in school and buried all her life into succeeding from then on in her school studies, music, school plays and speech contests. She soon made friends as she was able to be more confident.

       During this time, Lisa shut out of her mind that her parents were there, especially when her sister, Jill, went on to college. Yet she still tensed whenever Richard entered the room. There continued to be episodes from time to time, with Lisa's mother, as well. When Lisa begged for her mother's affection, Gail snarled at her and insulted her. Gail was not able to say anything positive to Lisa or give her any expression of love.

Chapter Twelve

The slap stung Lisa's mouth. It stung her mind and heart as well.

"You'll never amount to anything!" Lisa's father shouted.

Lisa and her parents were in a restaurant, eating soup. Nothing at all had been said before the slap and the shout. This was to be Lisa's farewell meal with her parents as they made their last stop on the way to Lisa's college.

Gail's face responded with a smirk of satisfaction as she witnessed the attack. How she seemed to enjoy it when Lisa's father made cruel remarks and hit Lisa!

"Is this all they can say to me as a good-bye?" Lisa thought. "They wanted me to go to college and achieve some goal with my music and other abilities, so why punish me with one last slap, verbal attack, and smirk?"

Lisa's heart sunk with severe pain and disappointment. What message were these people constantly trying to give her? At first, they wanted her to achieve something and then, they cursed any effort she might be making toward her goals! They were willing to take her to college. And yet, even though Lisa had said nothing, she was being given one last, cruel prediction about her future with a hateful scorn.

Lisa looked back in time to her memories of her father. She had never known him as a human being. She had only experienced him as a demon-possessed monster. Once in a while she wondered about him. Was there a person anywhere beneath the demons?

Then she thought of a moment when she had observed an unusual occurrence. She had been eleven-years-old, the same year she had been abused by Mr. Wiley. Lisa's father had opened a violin case and suddenly raised the violin to his chin and began to play. It was beautiful music with a full tone. Lisa was in awe. She was impressed with the power of expression in the instrument, which caused her to determine that one day she would learn to play it. She also saw, for the first and last time, a window into a soul that God had created. This was a person she had never seen before and would never see again.

Lisa asked her father where he had learned to play the violin. Then she waited for a reply.

"In the army", he said.

"How long did you take lessons?", she asked.

"For ten years", he replied.

Lisa was amazed that anyone could have had the opportunity to learn to play the violin and yet never pick it up and play it except on that one occasion. How could he have shut down his talent and continued his crazed behavior? Lisa had witnessed the most amazing peek into a soul hidden behind evil bondage.

Lisa also wondered about her mother's behavior. She suspected that Gail had been hypnotized by Richard at some point. Richard had been a hypnotist in the army and Gail had almost always seemed to be in a trance. She seemed unaware of most of the abuses performed by Richard on the children. His attempt to smother Lisa at age thirteen was one exception.

Looking back and slowly beginning to understand the pieces of her journey became one of Lisa's tasks. She struggled to make sense of her life and all that had occurred.

Another way Lisa had tried to make sense of her past was to reenact the abuses she had experienced by others through her own self-destructive behavior. She thought that harming her body in the same way others had afflicted her would bring understanding to her mind of why these things had occurred. These self-destructive patterns continued but the answers never came.

Chapter Thirteen

"I'll never get married!" Lisa had always said.

And she meant it. She was afraid of men and, as for having a family, she loved children. Yet she loved them so much that she did not want them to suffer as she had. Suffering was what life was all about for a child, Lisa thought.

As she pursued a career in Music Education, Lisa felt lonely, confused, and still focused on thoughts of suicide. She buried herself in her studies and ignored the other students most of the time.

Then Dan entered Lisa's life. He convinced her that marriage and children could be different than she expected. He also convinced her that she would be going against God's will if she did not marry him. So, after feeling she must obey Dan, she accepted his proposal and was very concerned that she would be able to be a good wife and mother.

Lisa wanted children, if life could somehow be different for them than it had been for her. Yet she sensed that she, herself, was still a child and did not know if she could give them what they might need from her.

Dan was abusive emotionally and sometimes physically to Lisa, even before marriage. Lisa thought this was normal and although it made her unhappy, she reasoned with herself that he was so much nicer than her parents, that it didn't really matter. Lisa thought this was as good as anyone could expect out of a relationship.

After her first child, Carrie, was born, Lisa struggled to thoroughly meet all of the baby's needs. She forced herself to hug the baby and to give her the love that she, herself, had never received. Lisa felt a painful mix of jealousy and depression. She longed for a mother just like herself to come and give her a hug also.

Depleted of energy and crying out to God for help to raise the child rightly, Lisa came to the end of her strength. She decided that she did not really know God any longer and was doomed to hell because He did not seem real to her anymore. She may have been suffering from Postpartum Depression on top of her usual depression.

Life was a constant struggle to meet the baby's needs. Lisa would conscientiously provide everything she believed Carrie needed, taking care of her and forgetting to take care of herself. Lisa grew weaker for she forgot to even feed herself. The baby was her only reality, while she fed Carrie balanced meals and vitamins.

There was a feeling of fire in Lisa's head at times, burning in her a torment she could only writhe in. It would seize her and make her cry out in pain. The feeling was emotional and yet Lisa could also feel it physically.

What was this agony? Lisa had felt it all her life, but others did not seem to experience this gnawing torment. Lisa would soon learn that things in the Bible concerning evil spirits were not only real, but had been living inside her tormented mind for her whole life. They had been binding her tightly to the damage her mind and emotions had experienced.

In the meantime, Dan and Lisa found a church where the people believed in performing the same ministries as Jesus had performed, in His name. This included healing and deliverance from demons.

Lisa had read about demons in the Bible but did not know what they were. She had always felt pressure to do things she did not want to do but she thought this struggle of forces inside her head was the normal course of life for everyone.

After Lisa had attended the church, the pastor's wife, Evelyn, came to visit her at her home. She had brought some information about deliverance from demons.

Lisa was crushed to think that if she had demons in her, this might mean that she was an evil person. Did it mean she belonged to the devil?

"No, Lisa, many things can cause demons to enter a person, including childhood trauma. It doesn't mean you are bad or even that you belong to the devil. God can deliver you from these things." Evelyn said.

Evelyn left a book with Lisa that explained more about this issue and Lisa was ready for the people at church to pray for her deliverance from demons. After a time of fasting and prayer that the church participated in, Lisa was ready to be prayed for. She cried out within herself to God to set her free. The pastor took authority in the name of Jesus for a "spirit of suicide" to leave.

Lisa felt something lift through her and out the top of her head. She felt different, somehow, and less tormented. She had never heard of or known that God could lift, from out of her, this oppressive force. The problems with suicide did not disappear because there was much healing needed from the things that influenced Lisa toward death, but a supernatural force was taken from her so she could begin to heal.

Lisa went home feeling empty and yet relieved as though a peace she had never felt in her life had come, a peace she felt she should have experienced all along. Yet she was puzzled about this experience. How was she a Christian and yet had never come out of any of the forces that had bound her for as long as she could remember?

Lisa was to experience a series of deliverance from demons. These demons, which had gained entrance through trauma and her reactions to the insecurities and defenses that she had developed through them, tried to control her behavior. Yet Lisa had a choice to stand against those urges, so she was not "possessed" as some people might use the term.

At another time, the spirit of "self-pity" left and Lisa could physically see details she had not seen before. The self-pity had been a "security blanket" to protect her from the lack of love from others. It was a substitute for "self-love" for Lisa could not love herself, yet someone needed to love her in order for her to survive. This was the way Lisa attempted to take care of herself.

There continued to be various types of demon spirits which had entered Lisa from the openings of past suffering. They were attached to the type of damage she had experienced.

One time, during a fight with Dan, Lisa was pushed over onto the floor and she could tell that her tail-bone had been broken. Lisa could not get up for a long time. Years later, the fracture was confirmed by x-rays at a chiropractic clinic.

Dan left and Lisa crawled out of her position on the floor. For weeks, she struggled to take care of her baby. She was in severe pain and grew ill. Every chance Lisa had to lie down and rest, she cried on and on, feeling very forsaken by God. Several times during this period of illness and pain, Lisa prayed to God, saying,

"God, I just don't feel important to you. I don't feel as though I am special to you."

The final core demon spirit, that Lisa had had all her life, was difficult to deliver her from because it was the only thing Lisa had ever known as her identity. "Rejection" had been her life. She was empty of all personal awareness of identity as the spirit of rejection left with a cry. However, right after that deliverance, a woman named Virginia, who clearly heard from God, came to Lisa and whispered into her ear,

"You *are* important to God! You *are* special to the Lord!"

Lisa had never told anyone of the prayer she had been praying to God. She knew this was a direct answer from Him.

Where would Lisa go from here? She had no idea who she was! Rejection was all she had ever known.

There was still the terrible hunger in Lisa's heart for love and without that "rejection spirit", there was just a void and still no love, no attachment to anyone. To whom did she belong?

Lisa had given her life to God and He was delivering her from demons. But she was not happy. If only someone would love her! The cry for parents was an insatiable thirst for Lisa. The people of her church were not understanding why she was not happy now that she had been delivered of so much.

"She must need to be delivered from more demons", they said.

Lisa was condemned by others for harboring demons, but Lisa knew that was not the problem. She needed healing within the depths of her heart and soul. There was something more that had happened to her than demons entering her through the trauma she had endured. There was deep hurt. There was a depth of damage that had been done to her mind. Trying to cast out more demons was ridiculous when this extreme healing was needed.

Several demons would try to return for years. Although Lisa stayed in prayer and reading the Bible, it was hard not to let them come back and oppress her. The wounds in her heart and her memories seemed to invite them to return.

The spirit of self-pity tried to return for several years. It had been a habit to allow that spirit to try to comfort her. Lisa prayed earnestly to God to show her how to conquer the oppression of self-pity which kept trying to gain entrance into her emotions.

Finally, a thought came into Lisa's mind which she sensed was a guidance from God. She had a plaque on her wall which quoted the prayer of Saint Francis which she felt directed by God to read aloud to herself every day. She did this for years. The self-pity began to fade away and eventually disappear. There came a time when Lisa would never be tempted again with self-pity.

The Prayer of Saint Francis

Lord, make me an instrument of Thy peace;
where there is hatred, let me sow love;
where there is injury, pardon;
where there is doubt, faith;
where there is despair, hope;
where there is darkness, light;
and where there is sadness, joy.
O Divine Master,
grant that I may not so much seek to be consoled as to console;
to be understood, as to understand;
to be loved, as to love;
for it is in giving that we receive,
it is in pardoning that we are pardoned,
and it is in dying that we are born to Eternal Life.
Amen.

During the time that Lisa remained at Faith Tabernacle, she began to take scriptures, particularly the psalms, and set them to music. As she played and sang them, a new place in her heart was formed for the scripture of the Bible. In place of the hatred, fear of condemnation, and ridicule she had felt from the Bible when her father had made her hear it in its cruel, twisted form, a new love for the Bible was growing in her.

Lisa played and sang psalm after comforting psalm and found other scriptures in Isaiah and throughout the Bible that expressed a love for children and for all who had been hurt and rejected by parents and friends. How the music redeemed and captured the words!

The references Lisa chose about God's love for children included:

"Can a woman forget her sucking child, that she should not have compassion on the son of her womb? Yea, they may forget, yet will I not forget thee." (Isaiah 49:15)

"Like as a father pitieth his children, so the Lord pitieth them that fear him. For he knoweth our frame; he remembereth that we are dust." (Psalm 103:13, 14)

"And they brought unto him also infants, that he would touch them; but when his disciples saw it, they rebuked them. But Jesus called them unto him, and said, Suffer (allow) little children to come unto me, and forbid them not: for of such is the kingdom of God. Verily I say unto you, whosoever shall not receive the kingdom of God as a little child shall in no wise enter therein." (Luke 18:15-17)

Some dealt with Lisa's self-esteem and depression:

"Why art thou cast down, O my soul? and why art thou disquieted within me? hope in God: for I shall yet praise him, who is the health of my countenance, and my God." (Psalm 43:5)

"But thou, O Lord, art a shield for me; my glory, and the lifter up of mine head." (Psalm 3:3)

Some developed a new sense of appreciation for these words as being from a *good* God:

"In God will I praise His word: In the Lord will I praise His word. In God have I put my trust: I will not be afraid what man can do unto me." (Psalm 56:10, 11)

"This book of the law shall not depart out of thy mouth; but thou shalt meditate therein day and night, that thou mayest observe to do according to all that is written therein: for then thou shalt make thy way prosperous, and then thou shalt have good success." (Joshua 1:8)

"Thy word is a lamp unto my feet, and a light unto my path." (Psalm 119:105)

Lisa's fear of the words of the Bible melted away the more she sang them. They were now words of healing rather than injury.

It would be later that Lisa's prayer life would be redeemed from the punishing way it had been used against her. She would discover that prayer had power to heal herself and others.

Also, during this time in her life, as Lisa struggled to keep the demonic oppression away and to communicate the healing that God was bringing inside of her, she wrote poetry. The words flowed and she would cry, releasing so much inward pain.

The poetry also was a way to connect with others by communicating her appreciation to them for whatever role they had played in her healing. Sometimes, Lisa would give people a copy of her poetry. Even the poetry, at times, would be misunderstood. People could not grasp from what level of Lisa's soul these words were coming. They interpreted them wrongly and according to their own suspicions or judgments.

Still the poetry continued to flow from Lisa as she faced each part of her journey toward mental health. It expressed painful feelings, yet many times ended with expressions of hope.

The desperate cry for parents to love her continued to grip Lisa and it seemed anyone who began to take that role would ultimately reject her. The pastors at Faith Tabernacle had been a support and yet anger arose one day, seemingly out of nowhere from Evelyn.

"You are depending on people!" Evelyn yelled at her.

Once again, Lisa felt so condemned for needing parents. She had always needed them and didn't know why it was a sin and why Evelyn would yell at her so! It frightened Lisa and she felt despair. Lisa would cry continually over this rejection for two years without stopping except when she slept. Continuing to care for her toddler, while crying, Lisa would forget to feed herself. She was exhausted from the tears and demands of taking care of Carrie, who turned two-years-old and then three-years-old while Lisa continued to cry. She would put Carrie in the stroller and walk for miles with her, crying the entire time she walked.

There would come a time when Lisa would finally need to be hospitalized. She had never been cared for concerning her emotional struggles since Dr. Carter had counseled her and arranged for her to be put on the anti-depressant. She had run out of her medicine when she went to college. There had been no professional treatment for her depression in all those years. Her first hospitalization would prove to be the beginning of a long struggle for wholeness.

Chapter Fourteen

"Lisa, why are you acting that way?!"

A critical voice was questioning Lisa. Although it was nearby, it seemed to come from far away.

Little Lisa was balled up on the floor against a hallway wall. The hall was filled with aides and with the other patients in the mental hospital, where Lisa had been kept for several months. Little Lisa was only being the same frightened two-year-old she had been many years ago.

"Why does she act like a child?"

"She must be trying to get attention!"

"Sometimes she seems like an adult and then she starts crying like a little baby."

"I think her tears are fake."

The critical voices continued to surround Lisa night and day as she struggled so hard to find relief and help. She did not know what those voices were trying to tell her. She was only being herself.

When Lisa had been first admitted to the hospital, she had her head down and could look at no one. She heard the nurses say to one another that she had not even developed basic trust that babies learn.

Lisa would not allow anyone to touch her. Her psychiatrist held out his hand to her, waiting for her to take hold of it when she was ready. After forming enough trust to allow the doctor to work with her, Lisa joined group therapy which he led. For some reason which Lisa did not understand, the doctor would yell at her during the group sessions.

Lisa only wanted to die. Why wouldn't they let her die?! They just wanted her to suffer. God, Himself, must be keeping her alive because he hated her and wanted her to be tortured. This is what she had always believed before her deliverance. Now, once again, it seemed to be true.

Lisa tried to find a way to end her life and was always stopped. For weeks at a time, a hospital staff member would follow her everywhere in the hospital to make sure she did not harm herself or else she was put in an I.C.U. room where she was kept locked up without any source with which to harm herself.

Lisa found out that the only way she might be able to escape life was if she could run away from the hospital. Lisa ran away several times but was always found. Finally, a disgusted staff person captured her, with the help of another, to bring her back to the hospital.

"If you are going to run off to kill yourself, sign out first so we won't be responsible for you!" the staff person complained.

The idea that Lisa could do this and take her life into her hands without being interfered with had never occurred to her. She immediately went to the nurse's station to ask for a form to sign out from the hospital. A nurse named Gretchen asked Lisa if she could talk with her first. She sat with Lisa long enough to find out why she had chosen to sign out of the hospital, gave her hope that somehow, someday she could be healed and talked her out of signing out.

There were many more hospitalizations for Lisa without anyone understanding why she could not get well. She would get temporary help, be released, and then, end up back in a hospital because of her suicidal behavior. She turned to counselor after counselor to find out what it was underneath the surface of her mind that she couldn't talk about or even think about.

Chapter Fifteen

During the time that Lisa sought counseling and had to be hospitalized several times again, she adopted a seven-year-old boy with many emotional problems. Although Lisa understood his emotional difficulties, she was not healed enough herself to always deal with the challenging behavior she encountered with her son.

Lisa loved DeWayne and tried as hard to be a good mother to him as she had with Carrie. Things were very stormy with DeWayne and also with her husband, Dan. Lisa spent most of her time devoting herself to her family and yet struggling severely with her past. It was after the birth of her third child, Isaac, that Lisa met Dwight. He was a counselor who had dealt with Satanic Ritual Abuse in the past.

Dwight recognized right away that Lisa talked as if there were more people inside of her instead of presenting just one personality. Memories began to resurface and Lisa was afraid to mention them to Dwight because she thought he would ridicule her and say that she made them up. They were strange memories that Lisa had never heard told before. Dwight who had studied about occult rituals would reassure her that she had not made them up because they were common practices in the occult.

Lisa joined a support group for those who had experienced severe trauma as children. Many of these new friends had also dissociated into separate parts to cope with their mental stress. For the first time in her life, Lisa found some people who actually understood her on a deeper level than she thought would ever be possible.

One day, during a group meeting, someone mentioned something about babies and Lisa lost control of her emotions. The memory of baby brother came back to her with shock. She began to cry uncontrollably. Somehow her mind had known only to release this memory when she had the support of her friends in the group to hold her and allow her to cry out her anguish. Yet for days after, she still lay in shock at home, with the memory of the killing and her false guilt concerning it.

Finally, the memory of Baby Brother's killing became more than Lisa could bear. Dwight suggested that the church Lisa attended at the time hold a memorial service for Baby Brother to help Lisa's memories heal. On a Sunday afternoon, a few of her friends met together to remember him. Lisa had written a letter to Baby Brother to explain to him how she had never wanted him to die. After a couple of friends sang "Jesus Loves Me", Lisa read her letter out loud.

As instructed by Dwight, the group, one by one, told Lisa that Baby Brother's death was not her fault. After praying together and blessing Lisa, the service ended. Lisa was surprised that a load had been lifted from her. The scars from this memory were to trouble Lisa to some degree for many years and yet, she noticed a dramatic change in the weight of the burden concerning this one trauma.

"Why would this memorial give me so much relief?", Lisa asked Dwight.

"You have been ritually abused." He answered, "Now you are being ritually healed."

Other memories surfaced too. Lisa remembered vaginal stabbings and being buried alive after the attempt to cut her heart out had been blundered. She also remembered being hung in a tree and then, taken down to watch other children die. Some of the rituals were designed to cause children to identify with death.

One by one, when Lisa's memories returned to her, she was afraid to tell Dwight that memory. She thought that neither he nor anyone else would believe such bizarre memories. Lisa did not even want to believe them herself. Yet Dwight confirmed to her concerning the studies he had made about Satanic Ritual Abuse that these things were common practices in the occult. In their own twisted way, the followers of Satanic worship had reasons these rituals were performed in the way they were.

Lisa would continue to struggle severely with memories and a strong sensitivity to other people's judgments and inability to understand her. So many people could not grasp what Lisa was going through. Her problems and struggles were very noticeable and yet not understood because her personalities would change and she would have flashbacks of her memories. Lisa would behave as a child and then, switch to a seemingly mature and wise adult personality. Even her husband had been puzzled and would remark that she would be a little girl one minute and "an old wise sage" the next.

Also, the depression had drained Lisa of her energy for the majority of her life. Was she rebellious of what was expected of her? Was she lazy? Unmotivated? Lacking the discipline to follow through? Why did she "daydream" and live somewhere in another world all of the time? Did she choose to put on an act for attention? Pity? Then what about her spiritual condition? Was she sinful and flawed in her character or spiritual interest? Not praying enough? Not reading her Bible?

"Why can't Lisa just lay things aside and start trusting God? Why wallow in such pits of depression and be so obsessed with death?" Lisa heard people say.

"Why doesn't Lisa think more positively? Everyone has problems but most seem to overcome them without wanting to take their own life?! It's not the end of the world!"

Or *would* it be the end for Lisa? While she heard judgments from others, she pulled away from them even more. She was even more isolated and cut off from them.

Lisa did not know any way to connect with other people. She had never learned how and now she found no way to be understood or accepted except rarely and for brief moments in time. These moments would end in more misunderstanding and rejection.

Lisa was lonely and despairing of being accepted. She was defensive for she felt she would lose any small bit of self-esteem if judged. Thus she was told that she was too sensitive. Why was she afraid of people's judgments? She was told that she shouldn't care what people think and yet she should take their unasked-for advise. With this frustrating barrier between Lisa and other people, how could she connect with them the way they told her that she should do?

Lisa was also told that suicidal tendencies are selfish. Yet Lisa believed that her death would make people happy. She was told that if she would try harder, she might fit in. Not being able to connect with others was *her* fault.

The religious world was the most critical of all. Many believe that emotional problems show a lack of faith in God. They believe that fear and depression are sins and that suicide must be the "unpardonable sin".

When Lisa seemed to be acting as a child, many people would criticize her. She would hear comments such as:

"The Bible says that you should 'put away childish things'."

This wasn't an exact or proper quote from the Bible, but another excuse to blame Lisa for acting as a child. Sometimes Lisa would retort .

"It also says to come to Jesus as a little child." she would say.

Many religious and mental health professionals would like to have straightened Lisa out and "shake her" into reality. What, for heaven's sakes, could be wrong with her?! However, for Lisa, this was life, the only way she had ever known it. She would love to have the energy to do the things that others could do and to be able to fit in with them. She had no way to picture how that could take place.

Besides all this, Lisa was thought to be critical and rebellious. She always seemed to be questioning authority. The truth was that Lisa was trying so hard to figure out life, people, and relationships. How were things really supposed to be? What was "abuse"? What was "normal behavior"?

Lisa changed quickly from one personality to another, baffling many people. But Lisa was baffled, too. Other people, authority figures as well, would also change quickly. They would seem kind and helpful one minute and then terribly cruel the next. Who could she trust if she had been able to trust at all?

After severe struggles, Dan and Lisa's marriage ended and Lisa was to raise Isaac by herself. She was lonely, but instead of needing a new husband, like Lisa thought, the cry for parents was what was really still overwhelming her heart. She continued to struggle with severe depression.

Continuing to seek help, Lisa mostly relied on her sessions with Dwight. Many painful memories and battles between the personalities that she had formed throughout her childhood constantly plagued and devastated her. This caused her nightmares for many years. Also, there was much fear and rejection in her relationships with people, especially parent figures.

Chapter Sixteen

All along, Lisa had difficulty relating to God because of her "father experiences". But what could she do about it? She had forgiven her parents but the gap in her life for them was still there.

Until God could provide some kind of human parenting for Lisa, she could not grasp the images described in the Bible of a "Heavenly Father" or of a caring, nurturing mother. According to the Bible, even evil fathers know how to give good gifts to their children (Luke 11:11-13). This meant that Lisa had not been fathered at all!

If God could not demonstrate His character to Lisa through human beings, how would she have a chance to develop or understand a "parent" kind of relationship with God? The process still depended upon available relationships of trust with people. Just like a child, Lisa was again at the mercy of other people to choose or not to choose to parent her. Now that her body was grown, it was even more difficult to find those who would fill this need in her life.

Much sorrow and disappointment would come to Lisa through the years. She would be shamed for her interest in father figures by being accused of sexual or romantic fantasies. Her hopes for a father's love were dashed again and again by people's judgments and betrayals.

Was Lisa flawed and evil to desire an affectionate father and mother? So many times throughout her life, people would tell her so in one way or another. This shame for needing love in ways that many others had received as young children would continue as Lisa was criticized for her delayed development in trust and social skills.

"You shouldn't need a father! God is your father!" People would scold.

"She is depending on people instead of God!" Lisa would hear them say.

What was "appropriate" or "inappropriate" in giving and receiving love? How could Lisa ever be understood and her longings be approved by others?

Many mixed messages were given to Lisa after she had become an adult. She was told not to be independent of others and not to need others at the same time. Should she need others or not?

Lisa still hungered for emotional care and love from parents. Parts of her seemed unable to grow up without that need being met. She was still a child in so many ways. She was told by some that it was "sick" for her to need parents at her age. They did not understand that she was more than one age at a time. Parts of her were stunted and had not been able to develop because of the deprivation of parental love.

Lisa tried desperately to learn how to connect with others. She did not know how to accept love and give it back to others in ways that both she and the objects of her love could understand.

"If only someone would love me!" Lisa cried.

At times the frustration and hunger for love would explode into tears as lava might erupt from a volcano. Other people would be concerned. Every so often, some people would sense her need. Either out of compassion for Lisa's need or else a desire to be a hero, they would take a parental role with her. They would promise to stay by her as she struggled for maturity but would ultimately end the relationship.

In spite of her misery, Lisa was able to teach music lessons. She would cry all day long with terrible hurt and memories. Yet one of the strong adult personalities Lisa had developed would come out to teach her students whenever they came to her home. No one could tell what kind of a day she had experienced.

Lisa also began to pray for others to be delivered from demons. This helped her to keep her own freedom.

The religious people in Lisa's life thought that the multiple personalities were demons. The mental health people thought that the demons were multiple personalities. Some believed in neither one. Lisa knew how to distinguish the one from the other.

Chapter Seventeen

The black automobile had become a comforting home for Little Lisa as Pastor Mark drove her to counseling and stayed with her to pray for her during the sessions in order to understand her needs. He showed her compassion and care for nine years.

Lisa had learned to trust this man through the years as he did so much to help her. She was being nurtured and not shamed for riding with him.

Pastor Mark's adopted children were usually with them. They were still at an acceptable age to need parents. Lisa liked to feel a part of the family. Perhaps she could grow up emotionally if she could continue to be accepted.

Lisa would talk to Pastor Mark the way she had chatted with Mr. Wiley years ago. However, this time she knew she would not be taken to vacant houses or have strange things done to her. He was truly a friend, meeting that need in her life for a father.

Pastor Mark's wife, Jane, also accepted Lisa and showed no signs of jealousy or suspicion. She had taken in many needy adopted and foster children. Lisa saw herself as just another "special needs" child. What better family to be a part of than one in which these needy children were cared for!

Lisa loved both Mark and Jane as parents and longed to honor them and make them happy. She had finally discovered parents who loved her.

Lisa's emotional problems were obvious and yet Mark and Jane seemed to accept her. Being part of that family meant everything to Lisa. Still, Lisa needed a commitment from them by having them reassure her that she could call them "Mom" and "Dad". Pastor Mark gave her that reassurance, saying that she was part of their family and would always be part of their family. She was told that calling them "Mom" and "Dad" would be an honor for them. Because of his permission, Lisa found the courage to address them in this way and express to them what their role in her life had meant to her.

Lisa's worst fear was being rejected by parents again. She had come so far in learning to accept her surrogate parent's love. To lose it now would be more than she could bear!

"I'm not your Dad!" Pastor Mark snarled at Lisa.

These were the words Lisa had feared the most and had hoped with all her heart that they would never come. Yet that dreaded day was here. The parental commitments were denied. Once again, Lisa would experience the deep pain of parental rejection.

Lisa's heart was stabbed by the cruel words. They went down to the roots of her existence. She knew that it was an attack upon her from beyond this world. It threatened to destroy everything that had brought her hope and healing for those nine years she had experienced Pastor Mark's compassion. Was this new blow possible for her to overcome? Lisa was now filled with the most desperate pain and hopeless anguish she had ever known.

Chapter Eighteen

What would become of Lisa's earnest struggle to survive and find emotional hope? All the complicated reasons Lisa had wanted to die came back in full intensity. How could Lisa bear this nightmare? Who could possibly comfort her from this ultimate rejection? Even the man who had won Lisa's trust and had helped her so much had announced that he would not keep the commitment that he had made.

Everything that Lisa had hoped and longed for was swept away from her. Moaning and crying she laid on her stomach in shock. The hollow place in her heart that had waited for parents was now filled with sorrow. What would become of her now? Would she be able to find hope to help her survive this devastation? No answers were within her grasp.

This rejection, along with the death of two friends, and having to leave her church was such an overwhelming loss. Back to her confusion and obsession with death, thinking that she should have died instead of her friends, Lisa lost all hope. This pain was worse than the stabbings, sexual abuse, and other tortures Lisa had endured as a child. She had, at last, learned to accept love and that love had been taken away from her.

Naturally, Lisa was back at the point she had been in her childhood of hopelessness and the thought that death was her only destiny. She had been taught this for so many years that the beliefs were thoroughly grooved into her mind. Being betrayed by so many brought back the belief that she was thoroughly unlovable and that people wanted her dead.

Becoming suicidal again only brought more frustration and fear to the people who did care for her. They abandoned her emotionally, not knowing what to do. They were convinced that she was better off without their counsel. As they began to push her away more, this led to a further sense of rejection for Lisa and an even stronger desire to die.

One thing that had also led Lisa toward suicide was that life was so bad, she thought death must be better, whatever "death" meant. Life was rejection. Every time life became a world of rejection for her, death seemed, once again, to be her purpose and destiny. People, in ignorance, pushing her away became a confirmation to her that she truly was the worthless being that she had been trained to believe she was.

Because of her strong desire for death and the devastation over the loss of her relationship with her surrogate parents, Lisa had to be hospitalized once again. Then she was put into partial hospitalization several more times.

She had met Carl, the psychologist, when she had been in partial hospital at other times. Eventually he became her personal counselor in the program as well. A new perspective about herself began to develop in her relationship of trust with Carl. He was not judgmental and had ideas for Lisa's self-esteem that would begin to turn her around from the despair she was in.

"Try to separate out the beliefs that 'they' taught you from new beliefs you are learning about yourself." he said to Lisa.

The trouble with this suggestion was that Lisa knew no other beliefs to believe about herself than what she had been taught. How would she know what was true?

Believing something new about herself was the only way Lisa would survive, so she took a piece of paper, drew a line down the middle, and wrote the things she had always believed about herself on the left side of the paper. On the right side of the paper she wrote what would be the opposites of those beliefs. Lisa had to be convinced somehow that those opposite beliefs were true about her. Carl coached her to try believing those things about herself that were on the right side of the paper. He also demonstrated to Lisa the truth of those affirmations by being her friend. She could not believe these new truths on her own.

Affirmations had always been helpful when she had used them during courses on self-esteem in the hospital. She was taught to create new beliefs about herself and read them out loud from 3x5 cards. She would improve as her mind began to receive the new messages about herself. But then, her mind would start to rebel against the new ideas as if they were a "foreign object". Then Lisa's suicidal behavior would worsen.

The old ideas were grooved into Lisa's mind. Anything foreign to those thoughts would be repelled by her mind. Though longing to be free from the old patterns, Lisa's mind had been prepared to cope with the world through false ideas. It would take much more than barely accepting the new truths about herself and reading them out loud for them to truly penetrate her mind and emotions. They had never been able to outweigh the ideas that Lisa had been brain-washed to believe. The repeating of these affirmations about herself were no match against the memories which steered Lisa toward thoughts of deserving death and suicidal wishes.

Lisa thought of a logical idea for literally erasing and reprogramming the "old tapes" in her mind. By taping new beliefs on her tape recorder and playing to herself these new truths as she was learning them, she counteracted the brainwashing she had received.

The thoughts and beliefs that had troubled Lisa were targeted and replaced specifically. These are examples of old beliefs and their replacement with new beliefs:

Old Belief: "I must die or others will be killed. People's deaths are my fault."
New Belief: "Lisa, by being alive, you help others to live well. You are innocent and free from blame."

Old Belief: "Parents rejected me, therefore I don't deserve parents who love me."
New Belief: "You deserve parents who love you. Even though you didn't have them, you still deserve them."

Old Belief: "People want me dead."
New Belief: "There are people who want you and love you. They need you and want you alive. Staying alive is a *good* thing to do."

Old Belief: "Because I was sexually abused, I need to be ashamed and to be punished by God."
New Belief: "You are pure and innocent. What others did to your body is not your fault."

Old Belief: "People think I am ugly."
New Belief: "Your body is beautiful in God's eyes."

Old Belief: "People won't want me unless I am seductive."
New Belief: "People love you for yourself. You do not need to find desperate ways to be wanted."

Old Belief: "If I let anyone be kind to me, they will be hurt or killed."
New belief: "Accepting love helps you *and* others."

Old Belief: "If I use my talents, I will be punished."
New Belief: "When you use your talents, you are giving a gift to others. You are doing nothing wrong."

These new beliefs were taped on a recorder. Lisa continued to add to the tapes every time her therapy revealed an old belief that was driving her back to rejection and suicide. Listening to these affirmations became her lifeline toward getting well. Her self-esteem was raised, slowly at first, and then, as she continued to speak to herself through the tapes, her image of herself and of her life began to be dramatically improved. Lisa had discovered a key to fight against the images of the past and their messages to her.

One of the things making it difficult for Lisa to form new beliefs about herself was how to distinguish truth from the falseness she had been taught as long as she still experienced the same words and treatment from others. Her past was only being reinforced by people in the present with their abusive attitudes toward her.

It took the help and influence of others treating her differently to challenge and begin to turn around the old thoughts that Lisa had accepted as truth for so many years. Over time, these influences gave her wisdom to record new affirmations. She had to listen to these recordings day and night to undo the damage of the old beliefs that were still controlling her mind.

The taped affirmations transformed Lisa's thinking, behavior, and mood every day. They helped her to fight against flashbacks and troublesome nightmares and against the damage her memories had done. Lisa would feel a new strength enter her mind and body as she listened to the affirmations.

Chapter Nineteen

Carl also began to teach Lisa about the "safe place". It would become another essential part of her healing.

"Think of a place of safety for you in your mind.", Carl indicated to her and the other members of the group.

Lisa tried to think if there had ever been a safe place for her at all throughout her life so far. The only one she could remember was the orange orchard grove where she had run away to as a child, which had only been safe for a few moments before she was found and punished.

That is when Carl taught Lisa that she could expand on this safe place in her own mind, making it safer and more comforting to her. She was to visualize the time she spent there being longer, adding more details there that she needed to make it safe and to make it pleasant.

The safe place became more and more beautiful. Lisa added water in the form of a peaceful stream, running through the land. The trees became larger than in the original orchard, producing more shade. The weather was calm, warm and peaceful with a gentle breeze as Lisa sat and sometimes laid down in a bed of clover and flowers.

Lisa built a large wall around the safe place, with a locked gate to keep her abusers out. As Lisa's mind continued to make the safe place more secure, birds begin to sing and chirp. There were squirrels and rabbits frolicking among bushes and trees. The sound of the water was very soothing and Lisa looked at it to calm her mind and emotions so they could continue to create more beauty in the safe place.

Lisa would learn to visit the safe place often, whenever she needed to feel more peaceful and secure. It would ground her into a stable place in her mind where she could be unafraid of her abusers hurting her.

Later, the safe place would be used continually by Lisa and her regular therapist, Mike, to give Lisa a place to start in and return to whenever dealing with the difficult memories she would have to process. It became a very important tool throughout her recovery.

Whenever experiences from Lisa's environment triggered her memories of trauma, Lisa could escape by thinking and writing more peaceful and beautiful images into the safe place.

Using a method of therapy called Eye Movement Desensitization and Reprocessing (EMDR), Mike had guided Larisa into her safe place. Then Larisa would invite other personalities into the safe place with her. The one who seemed the most damaged, suicidal, and disabled was Little Lisa, still bearing the memories of ages two and three.

With Larisa's coaching and nurturing and with Mike's suggestions during EMDR, Little Lisa began to come out of her fetal position and to make more and more movement within the safe place. She helped Larisa make the walls of the safe place more secure. Larisa would observe and encourage Little Lisa to make more progress during each session.

Larisa Dawn began to defend Little Lisa in her memories. She went into some of the memories where Little Lisa had taken much of the blame. She took the blame off of Little Lisa and placed it back upon her perpetrators.

Larisa desired to integrate as many of the personalities back into herself. "The Thinker" was the "Inner Self Helper" orchestrating the process of integration.

These parts had accomplished their purpose in helping Lisa to cope with traumatic memories. Instead of a sign of insanity, they served to keep Lisa sane. After recognizing that their purpose had been fulfilled, many personalities were willing to integrate back into the parts they had split from.

Some personalities would have their names changed. "Bad As Can Be" became "Good As Can Be". "Bad Girl" became "Good Girl". One of the personalities that associated sexual abuse with death changed her name to "Jewel", representing her value in place of the degradation and shame.

After gaining some self-respect, Lisa began to have a desire to care for her body. She had always believed that her body was created to be abused. Now she learned that it was an important part of her mission in life. Her body would be a channel to reach out and be a help to others.

Several new affirmations that Lisa added to her tape regarded the care of her body. Lisa would tell herself:

"You deserve to be protected, not abused. Cherish and protect your body. Take care of it. Protect it from harm. Protect it from abuse."

Lisa had a purpose. She would share her experiences and all that she had learned to benefit others, turning the bad into good. She would write about her safe place whenever she felt threatened by the outside world.

Writing became a resource for Lisa. It was like taking the stones off the altars where rituals had been performed on people and animals and, one by one, placing the stones on the ground. She formed the stones into words that would tell her story.

Chapter Twenty

Lisa began to imagine a house that had been securely built by a master builder. It was a stone house. Each stone had been fit together and designed to provide shelter for those who would live there.

But as Lisa observed the building in her mind, she saw parts of the roof detach themselves and run away during a storm. While the house was filling with water, the walls began to come apart. They would not stay joined at the corners for they did not want to lean on each other. The various stones began to crumble and betray one another. The foundation was broken by earthquakes, one shaken hope after another.

The house was family: fathers, mothers, brothers, and sisters. God, the Master Builder, had placed together the parts of the home so that no one would be left alone and unsheltered in the storms of life. All would experience the protection of love. Children would grow up and build houses of their own. The homes would be strong and secure with no parts missing. There would be belonging. Parents would know how to love their children for they, themselves, had been loved and sheltered.

But the structure of family was destroyed. Emotionally deprived orphans searched for love and belonging wherever they could find it. Groups that would use and control them, in trade for a false sense of belonging, would gather them into their midst. These groups were cults. They were not true family but a counterfeit.

Lisa had seen, through her study of the Bible, that the people of the church were meant to be a family to one another. According to some Bible references, members of the church were to be parents and siblings to one another. One other Bible verse, actually compared the people of the church to "living stones built together as a spiritual house"(1 Peter 2:5).

People had always expected the Master Builder to come down and be a family, all by Himself, to Lisa. Yet He had built the house for her and others to relate to one another. Now she felt left and deserted by the other stones. She had to believe in healing for her crumbled condition. She also must begin to look for

other stones to love and to hope for God to build a family for her
again.

Chapter Twenty-One

Lisa fell into the soft clover. There were velvet leaves with an assortment of purple, yellow, and pink blossoms. The water nearby sounded like gurgling bubbles, popping in the breeze. The leaves on the trees swept one another softly.

Peace settled down on Lisa's face, along with the warmth of the sun. Perfect calm surrounded the garden of trees and flowers.

Lisa knew there was a high, impenetrable barrier between herself and the outside world of evil people. She was in a place of peace.

The aroma of purple iris and pink peonies filled Lisa's nostrils and overwhelmed her sense of comfort. Her eyes gazed at the peaceful water, She heard the chattering of birds as they glided from tree to tree. As the breeze gently soothed her face, she tasted the lemon-flavored herb seeds as they wafted into her mouth.

Safe people were going to begin entering the safe place at Lisa's permission. Carl entered first. Lisa knew he was safe because he had never been judgmental to her. He had never expected anything except her innocence.

After Carl, Lisa's son, Isaac, entered, being relieved that his mother was safe and could pass more safety on to him. These two friends would not sabotage the safe place but would blend in with the beauty of the place.

Lisa touched the tender petals of a yellow lily and smiled. A green and brown bulrush plant rose up out of the water with its shoots bending as though bowing in prayer.

Lisa went over to the water to gaze at its beauty and saw her own reflection there. She blended in with the plants for she was a plant herself. She was a flower, a multi-colored flower, blending into this setting of peace.

Now ferns and small pines began to grow along the edge of the water, adding shade and green peace to the water. Here in the safe place were all the dreams Lisa had held in her heart for so many years. This was peace, sacred, soothing peace. Who could take it from her? Only those safe were allowed to enter.

Vines and flowers hung over the walls and hollyhocks stood guard all along the fence. There was purple, blue, and pink protection all around. This was the safe place where all parts of Lisa could escape to and develop.

As stated in the introduction, many names in this true story have been changed. This is to protect the identity of some and to bring objectivity and understanding for Lisa.

How is Lisa doing today? Every day is a new day of progress in the "safe place" as she integrates the various personalities. The affirmations renew her mind and soul concerning life. Each minute of Lisa's life, the false is being separated from the true. Each day is a new day of healing, just like drops of a cool rain might soak and soothe a burnt forest until it sprouts again.

Lisa is also like soil, being continually plowed so that new life can be planted and allowed to grow. She continues to adjust her mental and emotional eyes to the new light of a better day for her.

How do I know this? I am Lisa.

www.ingramcontent.com/pod-product-compliance
Lightning Source LLC
Chambersburg PA
CBHW051008060726

47593CB00017B/1270